friends

rule

...a very special book of friendship
especially for girls

Ashley Rice

Blue Mountain Press™

Boulder, Colorado

friends rule

Where would I be...
without you?

To:

Michelle

From:

Joy

Also by Ashley Rice

*girls rule ...a very special book
created especially for girls*

Library of Congress Control Number: 2003109923
ISBN: 0-88396-772-3

Certain trademarks are used under license.

Manufactured in the United States of America.

 This book is printed on recycled paper.

Blue Mountain Arts, Inc.

P.O. Box 4549, Boulder, Colorado 80306

I never would have gotten as far as I
have without the help of my
good friend. Never would have smiled
so much. Never would have laughed
so much. Never would have tried
so much. Or fallen-down-then-stood-up-tall
so much.

Never would have gotten this far
at all without the help of my
good friend. Never would have seen
the same grand things. Never
would have dreamt
the same big dreams.

And I never could forget
this friend
(you).

Friendship rules.

There are few friends quite like you...

you say things
that I care about...

you do things
that matter...

you make a difference
to me...

you make a difference
to other people, too...

and I know for a
fact that if you
were not here...

I wouldn't like the
world quite as much as
I do now.

You are my anchor

You are my anchor in this world
and in these rough and crazy seas.
When hearts and hopes
go down like ships,
you help me hold on to my dreams.
When other parts of me have gone,
you keep me going.
You keep me sane.
You are the treasure I love most,
like an umbrella in the rain.
You are my anchor in this world,
from here to as far as I
can see...

You are my anchor
in this world, and that
means everything
to me.

thou
art
beautiful

In my heart

You don't have to be perfect to belong
in this place. You don't need to have all
the answers, or   always know
the right thing   to say. You
can climb the   highest
mountain, if you   want. Or
quietly imagine   that you might,
someday. You can   take chances or
take safety nets,   make miracles
or make mistakes.   You don't have
to be composed at   all hours to be
strong here. You don't   have to be bold
or certain to be brave. You don't have to
have all the answers here, or even know
who you want to be...

       just take my hand
       and rest your heart
       and stay a while with me.

Friends forever:

Friends from the start, when
everything was new. Friends through
the hard parts of growing up we got
through. Friends
through the middle
parts: the good
and the bad.
Friends through
the happy times. Friends
through the sad. So wherever you go:
here, there, or wherever... know that
you've got a place in my heart —
friends from the start: friends forever.

best buds

Daisy chains

How do we pick our friends?...
Dearly, like gems. Carefully,
like flowers. The moments we
remember best stay with us
like a daisy chain; like a
necklace made of flowers,
worn with familiarity and love,
and close to the heart. We
arrange them until they
become something beautiful
and walk out into the world
holding hands.

Friend,

in all the people that I meet I
know that there will never be
another friend quite like you.

I believe in you

I believe in the way that you are
and the way you will be.
I believe in the things that you say.
You mean the world to me.
And if you should go,
if you should turn around one day,
if you should ever doubt your dreams
in any way,
don't think twice about it.
Don't worry too long
about whether you'll find a place
for yourself in the world — you belong.

I know that you'll get where
you're going someday.
For no matter what happens,
you will find a way.
I believe in the way that you are
and the way you will be.
You are a Shining Star
in this world...

    and you mean the world
        to me.

Whenever you need them...

The shirt
off my back...

the shoes
off my feet...

I'd give them
to you...

without missing
a beat.

?

Whenever you
need them...

whenever you
call...

my heart   and my hand

and my love: take them
                  all.

The shirt   my friendship
off my back...   to keep...

I'd give them to you,
without missing a beat.

Some days are rough

Some days
are rough.

Some days
are just hard,

and some days
are mixed-up.

Some days
never end.

but when it
gets tough

when you're
feeling disheartened

always
remember

that you've
got a friend...

in me.

Always time for

friendship

This is the dog
that ate my
homework.

These are the
letters I never
sent.

This is the laundry
I haven't done
yet.

These are the
words I never
said.

This is the bill
I haven't
paid yet.

"Things-I-will-
get-to": this is
the list.

You can't
count on the fact
that I'll always
do my housework
like clockwork...

but I
promise you
this...

You can forever
count on me as
a friend.

10 things I will never do:

1. I will never be too old to laugh at stupid jokes.

2. I will never be too busy to find time for special things that I think are important.

3. I will never wait in line for three hours in the rain.

4. I will never break a single person's heart, if I can help it.

5. I will never be too sophisticated to look for cloud shapes in the sky.

6. I will never be too skeptical to believe in dreams, or too jaded even to try.

7. I will never eat a vegetable dish I can't pronounce, unless there's a really good reason.

8. I will never be so preoccupied that I forget the day or season.

9. I will never forget all the times we got through.

10. I will never stop being friends with you.

A true friend

stays in your heart:

Distance cannot erase the
memory of your face from my
mind; for a true friend, once
found, is never forgotten, but
continues to change you, lives
on in your thoughts, and is
imprinted in your heart forever.

Friendship is
phone calls and letters
and going on through life
together.

I've found a friend in you:

For all the times you've
made me shine...

for all the funny
things you do...
for every time we've walked
so far...

and found a way

to make it through...
for every day you looked
my way...
for every moment that was true...

for every true word that you say...

I've found a friend in you.

True blue friends
are like sunshine...

best friends are always
a rainbow...

and friends like you?...
Well...

they're once
in a lifetime.

Definition of
a good friend:

A good friend is: someone who makes you smile. A good friend is: someone you're always happy to see. A good friend is: someone who is fun to hang around with, who listens, laughs, cares, shines, understands.

I think there should be an entry in the dictionary for the word(s) "good friend" (and then next to it, as the major example, could be your picture).

Friends like you
are hard to find.
In a lifetime, you get
only a few.
And when you find them,
you always know
them by sight and
by heart alone.
And when you find them,
you always grow
a little bit taller
in your soul.

And when you find
them, you also know
that, as the years
come, and as the years
go by...
that you have
been blessed just
to know them;
thus blessed am
I, thus lucky have
I been...
to know a friend
like you.

a friend...

like you is

like a rainbow

on a stormy

day or like a

flower growing

in the middle of

a city block or

maybe like

everyday magic...

(I don't know —
you're just pretty
cool.)

To my friend:

Everyone has people who are
important to them
in their daily lives.
But: looking back over the
years,
I cannot believe how many
times you stuck up for me,
stood by my side,
or helped me ride through
all the changes that
life brings.

You are so dear to me, my
friend... You stand by me and
understand. You are like a
star that guides my hand...
when I need it most. And
when I look back on all these
years of us being friends...
I wonder...
how would I ever have
gotten this far without you
beside me?

You are the best.

Life is confusing...

friends make it
easier to understand.

It's nice to know that
no matter where we are,
or what we are doing...
that at least one thing
(friendship) will always
stay the same.

Thanks for being a stable
part of my life.

There's nothing like a little
help from my friends.

There is no better friend
than the one who listens
to the end of all your stories,
good or bad...
who lends you an ear...
a locket...
a hand...

. . . and helps you fly.

You believed in me when
I wasn't that strong.

You held my hand.

You let me be wrong.

You laughed with me
when my jokes weren't
that funny, stood by me when

I had no money $.

You lent me your heart...

...You lent me your hand...

from the start, you were

my friend...

funny how life brings

us rainbows and very

special people when

we need them the most.

Necessary things
in life:

love

poe**try** ～
poetry

sunshine

books

♪ ♫
music

challenges

lip gloss

MTWTFS̈'s
Saturdays

bagels

pets

smiles

dreams

peace

cool shoes

a really good
pair of jeans

but most importantly...

friends

Hey friend:

When you came
my way...

it made a brighter
day for me...

thanks for
sharing your sunshine.

friends
make every day
more fun.

Peace.

May you find hope
and love and peace.
May your journey be safe
and your dreams
without end.
May you sleep under stars
and live in days of good
fortune.
And may you always
walk among friends.

Nothing compares to your
style, your smile, or
your friendship.

Sometimes I wonder if you know how wonderful you are, or if being wonderful is one of those things that somebody has to tell you about, like when everyone is talking about how beautiful this one person is and that one person is the only one who doesn't know.

Maybe you already know how wonderful you are on the inside, but as your friend, I just wanted to tell you that this wonderfulness of yours...

it shows.

In the end,
friends are what
matter most...
the years, the
tears, the smiles,
☺
the miles...

...and all the things
that happened
while we were out
there chasing
our dreams.

Friends rule.

You are
    my angel

You are my angel
when I'm down.
You make me smile
when I am frowning.
You are my angel
when I'm glad.
You are right there
by my side.
When I laugh
or when I cry,
you are an angel
in my eyes.
You are my angel...

and I just wanted
    to say thanks.

Friends are angels sent
down to earth to make
good days and to help
us find our way.

A friendship flower:

 You would think
that we might have
forgotten each other
by now; life is so
uncertain — so many
people come and go,
like rain. But no
matter where I have
stood, or what
roads I've been
down, you have
been there for
me — at every turn,
along the way...

...and I guess
that some things
change and other
things don't
and there are
some special
types of
friendships that
grow and yet stay
the same. And
I'm just really
glad we've got
that special sort
of friendship... that
is there for you;
there for you
always.

I'll be there for you

If you've got secrets you want to tell, we can talk all day long. If your dreams get broken somehow, I'll remind you that you belong. If you need someplace to hide, you can hold my hand for a while. If your sky begins to fall, I'll stay with you 'til you smile.

Whenever you need some space, there's my room — you can take it. If someone breaks your heart, together we'll unbreak it. When you feel sad or empty inside, I'll show you you're not alone. If you get lost out there, I'll come and take you home. I'll go with you somewhere else, when you need to get away. And when nothing seems to be going right, and you need a friend...

I'll stay.

I forget a lot
of things...

My wallet, for instance...
or where I last put
my good set of keys.

I forget addresses
and phone numbers, and
sometimes I even forget
    the date.

I forget a lot
of things, and I
will forget a lot more
before this life is through.

But one thing I know
for sure, my friend...

...I will never forget you.

The Friendship Pages...

Just a few words about my friend, _____.
name

♥   ♥   ♥   ♥   ♥   ♥   ♥

What I like best about you is...

_____
_____
_____
_____

What I've learned from you is...

_____
_____
_____
_____

What I will always remember about you is...

_____
_____
_____
_____

The songs that remind me of you are...

_____
_____
_____

The animal that makes me think of you is...

_____
_____

A place to keep
your favorite friends'
addresses and phone numbers:

Name:_____

Address:_____

_____

Phone:_____

E-mail address:_____

Name:_____

Address:_____

_____

Phone:_____

E-mail address:_____

Name:_____

Address:_____

_____

Phone:_____

E-mail address:_____

Name:_____

Address:_____

_____

Phone:_____

E-mail address:_____

Name:_____

Address:_____

_____

Phone:_____

E-mail address:_____

A place to
write your favorite
friend memories:

Remember when...

_____
_____
_____
_____
_____
_____
_____
_____
_____
_____
_____
_____
_____
_____
_____
_____
_____
_____
_____
_____
_____
_____

A place to paste your
favorite friend photos:

Take this little book
and put it someplace
special so that every
time you look at it
you will remember just
how special you are...

and just how much
your friendship means
to me.